TEA TIME WITH JOY

- *A Revelation on Women's Influence* -

Joy Gayle Graeter

Unless otherwise indicated, all Scripture quotations are taken from the NKJV Bible. Copyright © 1988 by Thomas Nelson, Inc. Used by permission.

Tea Time with Joy

ISBN: 978-0-692-24175-2

Library of Congress Control Number: 2014914195

Copyright © 2014

Published by Joy Ministries International

PO Box 51057
Colorado Springs, CO 80949

http://www.joyministriesintl.org/

Prepared for publishing by: Orion Productions, LLC.

PO Box 51194
Colorado Springs, CO 80949

www.orion316.tv

Editor: Daphne Parsekian

Printed in the United States of America. This book or parts thereof may not be reproduced in any form, stored in a retrieval system, or transmitted in any form by any means—electronic, mechanical, photocopy, recording, or otherwise—without prior written permission from the Publisher.

With special thanks to:

Meagan Ward, *Front Cover Artist*

Ann Bookout

Beth Landt

Rita Wolf

Partners

Board Members

Joy Ministries International would not have been able to grow or minister without the dedication and participation of people with vision. I appreciate everyone who has blessed this ministry with their prayers, love, funding and time. Your encouragement and input have made all this possible.

My love & blessings,

Joy

Contents

Foreword
Page 9

Preface
Page 11

Chapter 1 The Revelation
Page 15

Chapter 2 Who Are We as Women?
Page 25

Chapter 3 Who Is Jesus Christ to Us?
Page 37

Chapter 4 What Changed for Us at the Cross?
Page 47

Chapter 5 What Is Total Reconciliation?
Page 55

Chapter 6 How Do We Get Started?
Page 59

The End
Page 71

Foreword

God hides things for us, not from us. Joy has successfully brought us through her revelation of what a woman of God truly is through her new book, *Tea Time with Joy*. She has walked out this journey personally from being a part of the "herd on Hughes Street" to ministering the Word of God to men and women desperate to know Him. The Lord has revealed to Joy how character is instilled in children, which is "at the knees of their mothers, grandmothers and aunts." What a profound revelation this is for women if we can use our spiritual authority to rebuild the "family," the institution that God created and loves. I have been privileged to watch Joy grow in her relationship with the Lord. She can earnestly say, "I know in whom I believe and what He thinks of me!" I highly recommend this book if you hunger to understand who women really are in the Kingdom of God.

Beth Landt

Dean of Women
Charis Bible College

Preface

As I sat in my comfy chair on a cold morning in 2010, some scriptures from the books of Esther and Ruth came alive to me. I asked myself, "How could these thirteen to sixteen-year-old girls have such depth of character, poise and wisdom? Who had taught them? Wasn't Esther an orphan? Wasn't Ruth a widow and an idolater?" The questions went on until I finally asked the Lord about them. Then an amazing revelation began to open up to me, and I was inspired to write this book. The seed for *Tea Time with Joy* was planted in my heart.

Little did I know this inspiration would pull me along spiritually as though I was on a conveyor belt. On and on it moved me forward while continuing to enlarge and develop as I prayed and sought the Lord. My relationship with Him grew as I began to understand His love for me and humanity. I saw through this love, from the very beginning in the garden, that He established order and principles for us to live by. These are still in effect today. Esther and Ruth walked in these principles and had favor with God and man.

At the beginning of my study, the focus was on women during the time of Esther and Ruth, but later it changed to the women of today. There are both differences and similarities in the roles women played in society both then and now. It is my purpose with *Tea Time with Joy* to explore these differences and similarities. The wonderful and powerful role Christian women have in the world today could influence their home, community, career and church in a positive way. God empowered us in the garden with this gift of influence. It is my firm belief that we can use this gifting to influence everything around us for good! All we must do is see the possibilities and act!

First, we must know who we are in Christ. With this knowledge, we can confidently move within our spheres, strengthening and encouraging others all around us. Just as Paul said in Philippians 3:13, we, too, must forget the way things have been in the past and move forward into the high calling we have in Christ! It doesn't matter if we've done things wrong in the past. We can move into tomorrow with new purpose and focus.

Come, let us sit together and have a cup of tea as we explore the revelation God gave me. The role we have as women will open up as the revelation of our influence unfolds before you as it has to me. Let's begin now.

Chapter 1

The Revelation

As I begin with the explanation of this revelation, see it as a tiny seed being planted in your heart. Before long, it will expand and grow into a plant so big it will fill your land. Initially, I understood it to relate only to the children in my life. Then it began to grow, and soon I saw it applying to every age of mankind around me. This revelation of influence is amazing.

In the first two chapters of Esther, we see events happen that allowed many young girls to be chosen to go before the king. Queen Vashti's offensive behavior toward the king made this opportunity possible for these girls. Esther was among those chosen to be taken to the palace and placed under the care of Hegai, the custodian of the women. He was the eunuch of the palace.

From the beginning, he favored Esther. This was God's blessing on her. This favor would help her fulfill God's purpose in her life and the lives of the other Jews she would rescue. When reading this, we must remember Esther was quite young, but the way she handled herself made her seem very mature. Her character traits became evident as she was challenged in many different ways while waiting for her audience with the King. She was patient and longsuffering as she was beautified and bathed in oils for a year prior to her meeting with him. She was humble and able to adapt well to her new surroundings. Few women could have done that. Because of her relationship with God, she was able to walk in wisdom and rely on His help in her situation despite her youth.

When I questioned God as to how Esther's character had been formed and instilled in her, He seemed to speak to my heart and say, "At the knees of her mother, grandmother and aunt." This statement sent me on a quest to find out about this. I found in Jewish tradition that the teaching and training of children was left mainly to the women. Therefore, someone other than Mordecai would have instructed Esther in her duties. Her training would have been turned over to someone in his household, possibly a grandmother or aunt. She would have been trained to honor, to live with dignity and to serve others.

The Revelation

This training prepared her for the role she would play as she fulfilled God's will for her life. Mordecai's role where she was concerned was one of financial covering and protection. As she was being challenged during her stay at the palace, he helped her remain steady. He reminded her of her duty to save the Jews in the region by entreating the king on their behalf. His help to her was invaluable.

With further study of the Word, we see Ruth had characteristics similar to Esther. She was submissive and obedient to those who had charge over her. Both girls were willing to lay down their lives and risk everything to fulfill their purpose. They are wonderful examples of those having a relationship with and faith toward God.

Similarly, they had difficult times in their early years. Esther was orphaned and Jewish, and Ruth was a Moabite idol worshipper. Esther's training from the women around her guided her to honor God, herself and Mordecai, while Ruth's training led her to honor God, Naomi and Boaz. With their outstanding character, not only did they bless their own generation, but they have continued to bless every generation through the centuries.

Though women in this period of history influenced primarily children and adolescents, they also taught younger women how to be wives and mothers. Regardless of their nationality or geographic region, women's influence was everywhere throughout the earth. Like Esther and Ruth, our character speaks to everyone around us. As women, we influence the generations as we train them at our knees when they are children and then later on in their relationships when they are adults. Our godly influence has a positive effect on them throughout their lives. Whether they are young or old, we influence mankind. Just as Esther and Ruth were influenced by women working with them and involving them in everyday activities, we can do the same.

As we observe children playing in various settings, at home, at school and at church, it becomes evident their play is more than mere play. **Children are acting out real-life struggles on a small and very manageable scale.** They express themselves with unharnessed emotions. In their play, they kick, pinch, throw things, refuse to share, scream, pull hair and hit. It is during these times that they should be guided toward Jesus. This is a time of great opportunity to move them from selfishness to honor, dignity and service. We can introduce them to grace at this point, and mercy can enter into their relationships. Life can be managed here so it won't get out of hand later on when they are adolescents.

As a mother watches her children play, she can guide them to the proper, godly conclusion in their interaction with others. Respect for themselves and others can develop with harmony and peace being the result. The goal is that they grow up to honor their mother, their father, their playmates and, ultimately, God. It won't be very difficult for them to see God after they have been guided to honor those in authority in their lives on a daily basis. It becomes a natural and normal way of thinking. Children guided in this consistent and loving way will come to know God more easily.

The training ground at the knee is the "golden time." A woman's great influence and power is untapped in families today for the most part. We are so busy with work outside the home or other distractions it's hard for us to focus on our child's playtime. Because of these distractions, our value and importance in this role is unrecognized by ourselves and others. We don't realize we should be the major influence of the next generation. Unless a big change occurs, the guidance and influence needed in lives today will continue to be left up to others that are not anointed for the task. Babysitters and guidance counselors can't do what we have been designed by God to do. Their understanding and ability is limited.

It's the lack of godly influence in their lives that makes the difference. When we interact with them at the adult level, we speak into their lives using God's principles. These principles can be used to establish stability at any age. Young women must be taught to honor their husbands and love their children. This is very difficult to teach at this time in history because of the destructive forces arrayed against the family unit. But, it's not impossible. It depends on the relationship the woman has with Jesus. That makes all the difference in the result.

Our influence starts at the knee with children and continues as we involve ourselves with men and women of every age. We can see many lives changed for good around us. Here is an example from my life of a wonderful Christian woman named Ollie whose influence helped guide me to Jesus.

I was only four years old at the beginning of our relationship. The town where I lived was in the South, and there were not many opportunities

The Revelation

for blacks to work there. In fact, they had to have a written permit to work in our town at that time. It was then that my mom made friends with Ollie. How this came about, I'm not sure. But, they must have become close because Mom trusted her with me.

My first meeting with Ollie that I recall, Mom took me by the hand and walked me to the end of the sidewalk in front of our house. We stood watching a small black woman walk up the hill on the other side of the street from the bus stop. There was little traffic on our street, so when Ollie was directly across from us, Mom let go of my hand and told me to go to her. I walked across the street and put my hand in Ollie's. We walked to the house where she was employed as a maid, and I stayed with her for what seemed like the whole day. It was probably only about an hour or so though. She sang hymns, danced and laughed. She told me about Jesus! When she sat me in her lap, I rubbed my hand up and down her black arm. Then I would look at my hand to see if any of her color had rubbed off on me. She would laugh so hard at this her stomach would jiggle.

Ollie's favorite name for me was Angel Baby. She called me this even after I was an adult. Although I can only remember a few details of these times, I know I spent many hours with her at the house where she worked. Her laughter and joy were infectious. Her influence drew me closer to knowing Jesus. It also helped me deal with the racism that was all around me growing up in the South. She dared to cross the racial boundaries. Her faithfulness to Jesus and her loving touch have continued to bless me throughout my life. She was a part of my life until after I was married. When my first child was born, my husband and I moved away to another state, and I lost touch with her. What would I have done without her influence?

There are children all around us who need our touch. A simple pat on the head, a kind word, or a loving smile could turn them from sadness to joy. Consider my story of Ollie when the opportunity presents itself. We are ambassadors of Jesus in this world. In order for us to understand how far-reaching and necessary this gift of influence is, we must ask ourselves some key questions. Some of the answers to these questions might overlap a bit from chapter to chapter. Let's ask questions such as:

- Who are we as women?
- Who is Jesus Christ to us?

- What changed at the cross for us?
- What is total reconciliation?
- How do we get started influencing within our spheres?

Now that we have been "seeded" with the revelation of our influence, let's "water" it as we ponder its possibilities. Unless we understand the great need for this gift of influence or how it can work in our lives, there is a danger of our falling back into complacency. We must see it as the way God intended for us to operate. Yes, we are busy, and we have many obligations in our lives. However, the vision of our influence is in God's heart, so it should be in ours also. Let's see in the next chapters where these questions take us.

Proverbs 29:18a NKJV:

"Where there is no revelation, the people cast off restraint."

Chapter 2

Who Are We as Women?

As we investigate this question, we will begin to see how and where we have misunderstood our position. Currently, the role we play in life is somewhat different than God intended it to be. Let's explore this question from His viewpoint.

In the garden, in the very beginning, God created Eve as Adam's helpmeet. She wasn't his servant. She lived at his side as a counselor and advisor. Her value and identity were the same as his. She was, after all, bone of his bone and flesh of his flesh. She was not in a position higher or lower than he. She fit beside him in a place of honor. In Genesis 1:26–28, we read where both Adam and Eve had dominion over things on the earth. Both of them received the instructions about this directly from God. They were on equal footing, apple to apple.

However, today, women see themselves more like a grapefruit than an apple. Eve differed in size, strength and purpose, but there was no difference of power in the spirit. In the Spirit, they were neither male nor female. They were totally comparable. Women's minds have been permeated with the lie that they are less important and less capable than men because of the Fall and the part Eve played in it.

This is the point that confuses us today. We haven't seen ourselves on the same footing with men. Society has defined and redefined woman's role many times...it seems the main thing in people's minds through the years has been to keep us under control. Most of the time, we have been depicted as a threat to man and incapable of handling our emotions. Our place in the church has been narrowly defined to working with children and serving meals, with only a few opportunities to speak from the pulpit.

But, how does God see us? He sees women as vessels He will use to promote health, balance and strength in the overall family unit, His church and the world. In these arenas, we must use our influence for good. Woman is the key component in nurturing people of any age, from babies to the elderly. Our ability to adjust and adapt is needed in order to deal with mankind on multiple fronts. From the kitchen to the board room, we must meet the challenges with skill and grace. In a sense, our skill in running the home can be compared to running a small corporation. We schedule, plan, budget, make projections for future growth, make travel arrangements and plan events. We are amazing!

Let us embrace the revelation of our role of influence with great joy and expectation from the Lord. We have been stagnant long enough! Satan knew if he was successful in tempting Eve, she would turn and use her influence (then perverted) to tempt Adam. Through the centuries, this has resulted in confusion and mistrust between men and women. In the mind of God, there is no war between the sexes or confusion of sexual orientation! Both men and women have their place and purpose in the earth, and both are necessary! Man isn't our problem, ladies. It's the hidden parts in our own soul, the areas we can't see. We must be willing to face these areas in order to start the process of setting ourselves free to influence as God intended. We are valuable, creative creatures.

Proverbs 31:10b NKJV says:

"Her value is far above rubies."

Like Eve, we are powerful, anointed beings. However, the gift of influence in its perverted state has been used by many in evil ways. Manipulation is perverted influence. We must be careful to make sure we are using godly influence and not ungodly manipulation. We have been maligned in man's eyes because of those who use it wrongly. Whether we are young or old, this gifting of influence is within us, and some might say it increases with age. As homemakers and career women, this gifting can affect everything around us. With it, every aspect of our life can be brought to a higher level.

In recent years, manipulation by the media through Hollywood and the feminist movement has had far too much latitude in defining our role as women. These voices of the world have strongly suggested what we wear, how we fix our hair and how we visualize ourselves as women. It has determined at what age our usefulness is seemingly diminished, and the feminists have influenced us in the way we treat the men and children in our lives. Little by little, this movement convinced us we were missing out on life's best; that men were our enemy; and children could be aborted without consequence.

These ideas came from the devil himself. They attack the foundation of the home by undermining the strength of both the role of mother and father. We must use the Bible as the only true source for defining these roles. As Christian women, we should rise up and take our rightful places and help others to do the same. No longer can we afford to let Hollywood, the media, the feminists, or the world around us determine how we feel about ourselves, our lives, or our futures. We have someone wonderful to present to people—Jesus Christ! As we develop our relationship with Him, we become stronger and more adept in our ability to take back areas the enemy has stolen from us. We have much to do in order to repair the damage that has been done. **Our goal is to learn who we are in Christ, how we influence and how we can confidently rest in our re-established role.** We have everything we need to accomplish this. Let's begin by looking to the Scriptures for guidance.

Starting with Proverbs 31:10–31, we see a woman moving through her life with confidence. She sees to the needs of others, and her husband's heart safely trusts in her. She does him good all the days of her life, and she has no lack of gain. She tends to business by buying a field and planting it; she influences the local market to buy her goods; she is praised in the gates! Even her husband praises her, and her children rise up and bless her.

When reading these scriptures in the past, we have felt very inadequate, even condemned. We didn't see how we could ever be as she was. But now, with a new understanding of our place and role in society, we can see that Proverbs 31 reveals how God sees the women who have come to know Him. We are this woman! We are the righteousness of God in Christ Jesus according to 2 Corinthians 5:21. We are "virtuous" and capable already! God isn't waiting for us to be good enough. He sees us seated in heavenly places in Christ Jesus right now according to Ephesians 2:6.

His perspective of us is based in truth, while ours is based on what we see and feel. The fact is, we are held captive by a body of flesh in this earth. His Truth always trumps our fact though. We must let our current perspective change as we study the Scriptures.

Unless this change occurs, we will continue to judge the spiritual things in our lives incorrectly. His viewpoint of us is all that really matters. He sees us as the head and not the tail, and we are over and not under every situation according to Deuteronomy 28:13. It says we are the kings and priests in His kingdom in Revelation 1:6, who are able to speak to the mountains in our lives and cast them into the sea with faith-filled words as in Matthew 17:20. His view of us is so much better than our earthly view. Let's continue to hold His Word above what we see with our eyes or feel emotionally.

There is another piece to the process of gaining our freedom. God tells us in His Word to submit to others. Humility is the fuel that moves us forward to our renewal, while pride stops any forward progress.

Isaiah 54: 2–3 NKJV says:

"Enlarge the place of your tent, and let them stretch out the curtains to your dwelling. Do not spare; lengthen your cords, and strengthen your stakes.

For you shall expand to the right and to the left, and your descendants will inherit the nations, and make the desolate cities inhabited."

"You" is the subject of the first sentence of this scripture. It commands us to enlarge the area of our tent. God has put a plan in place to do this through His Word and godly friends. It's a picture of how the Body of Christ works. Since curtains and blind spots are in everyone's soul, it takes the Word and godly people to reveal them to us. We must learn to hear from those whom God sends our way. Without these people and His Word, we would remain in darkness.

Curtains restrict the light in our dwellings. They come in various thicknesses. Some are so thick light cannot penetrate at all. This causes blindness in the way we think and feel about things. God wants us to look at the interior of our souls, the mind, the will and the emotions. He wants the light of His Word to guide and heal us there. As these filters or curtains are identified, they begin to move out of the way. Then God's light penetrates, and revelation comes where darkness had been. We begin to see who we truly are as women. Here is a simple illustration of a filter in my life.

I went to the store to buy groceries. While I was there, I wanted to pick out a gourmet coffee. A gentleman was at the coffee display, and we discussed which brand was the best. I chose one, went home and put away all the groceries as usual. A few days later I had finished the can of coffee I had been using and went to the pantry to get the gourmet coffee. I couldn't find it there. I looked everywhere for it. The coffee wasn't to be found. Then as I was walking down the hallway later that day, I heard the Lord say to me, "Joy, it wasn't a can. It was a bag!" I turned and went directly to the pantry. There it was. A "bag" of coffee on the shelf exactly where I had put it!

You see, the curtain in my mind was a "coffee filter"! I had always bought coffee in a can, so that's what I automatically looked for. Similar filters are in everyone's thinking, and only the light of revelation can remove them. They seem normal to us. But, as the curtains are drawn back and as light comes in, we actually begin to see what is really there. Obstacles have been in our paths all our lives, and we have simply put up with them in the darkness. For us to grow past the familiar curtains in our Christian walk, we must let others' insight and God's Word enlighten us. We are in control of this, of course. Our permission is necessary. The people we allow to influence us spiritually should have proven character and the fruit of the Holy Spirit in their lives. As their help comes to us, we must choose to keep the cord drawn back and tied to the stake so the curtains remain open to the glorious light of freedom.

There are thought patterns or boxes in our minds that we operate from most of the time. For years we have allowed public opinion, tradition, bad church doctrine and ignorance to keep us from peeping out of these enclosures. Womanhood has long suffered in silence within these confines, resigned to their limitations. In a sense, we have agreed to these restraints with few exceptions. Now, as the light of

God's Word breaks into these veiled partitions, we can fulfill our roles as women. It isn't a matter of man against woman or young against old. We are not at war with anyone else. The war is between our own ears—in our own minds. By removing the mountains in our minds, we clear the path for God's Word to work. This is where we begin by exercising our authority as believers.

We have much unchallenged "chatter" in our minds. Up until now, we have gone along with whatever crossed our minds, accepting it as truth. We never considered slowing our thoughts down and challenging them as to whether they lined up with the Word of God or not. Usually, we let them float through without opposition. By our doing so, the devil had success in deceiving us. But now, we can slow them down, look at them and cast down whatever does not line up with the Word of God. Thought by thought, we can take authority over this part of our souls and free ourselves from these restrictive boxes.

Ephesians 6:12 NKJV:

"For we do not wrestle against flesh and blood, but against principalities, against powers, against the rulers of the darkness of this age, against spiritual hosts of

wickedness in heavenly places."

Our mind is the creative and imaginative part of the soul. It is here that we "see" and believe whether something is truth or a lie. The ruler of darkness, the devil, puts ungodly thoughts in our minds, and we believe them as truth until revelation on the Word comes. This is the process of renewing of the mind by the Word, as stated in Romans 12:2. Dealing with these old ways of thinking is difficult as first, but necessary. It's a tedious process, but in time, peace will replace fear and unrest. No longer can we afford to walk as downcast, silenced and banned women. We have a gift from our Father God that is wonderful, useful and needed in our world today.

We must walk in our freedom as powerful, godly influencers. As long as the enemy can keep us isolated and separated within, our effectiveness is diminished in the world. At first, we are not used to light in these areas. But, as we grow accustomed to "seeing" differently, we begin to enlarge. Our spheres are growing, and we are learning more about the areas we can influence. God expects us to see and hear His ways.

Matthew 13:16 NKJV:

"But blessed are your eyes for they see, and your ears for they hear."

We want to see and to hear as He directs us. We must come out from behind our curtains, throw our leg over the side of the enclosure and shimmy down the outside to freedom! Remember what a wonderful feeling you had the first time you walked into a new, spacious home after living in cramped quarters? Our experience of spiritual freedom is similar. God has "upgrades" for us to enjoy in His kingdom. We move and grow from glory to glory, faith to faith. We're increasing as we purpose to allow light into darkened areas and lengthen our cords and strengthen our stakes.

Chapter 3

Who Is Jesus Christ to Us?

Jesus is so many things to us. At first, we know Him as our Savior. Many of us have been born again since childhood, so the names Savior, Redeemer and Lord are familiar to us. With research, we find out those names are inclusive and contain many other meanings, such as Healer, Friend, Deliverer, Counselor, Baptizer and Provider. We are less familiar with these. He is the beginning and the end, the Alpha and Omega. By the Holy Spirit we are enlightened and given understanding of each aspect of these names. Because it will take us a lifetime of relationship to realize we have only scratched the surface of His depths, we need the Holy Spirit interpreting the Word and giving us revelation knowledge.

Isaiah 55:8–9 NKJV:

"For My thoughts are not your thoughts, nor are your

ways My ways," says the Lord. "For as the heavens are higher than the earth, so are My ways higher than your ways, and My thoughts than your thoughts."

Jesus related to man directly, face to face, when He was on the earth. Today He relates to us through the Holy Spirit. In order to get revelation of Jesus' other names, we need to understand the role the Holy Spirit plays in revealing them to us. He was sent by Jesus to the church in Jerusalem after the crucifixion. Jesus told His followers to tarry in Jerusalem until the Holy Spirit came with power from on high. On the Day of Pentecost, they were all filled with the Holy Spirit and endued with power just as Jesus had promised. They all spoke with other tongues and did mighty miracles for the Lord as a result. Healings such as blind eyes opening, deaf ears hearing and the dead being raised to life were made possible with the power of this gift. Jesus the Healer was glorified as the Holy Spirit operated through the believers in Acts 2:1–47. The followers in Jerusalem, men and women, began to influence everyone around them in a positive way. It's the same for us today. Our influence will increase with the power of the Holy Spirit operating through us.

The Holy Spirit is called the helper, the comforter. We go through phases in our lives when we are

Who Is Jesus Christ to Us?

desperate and in need of a helper or comforter. We usually try to focus on prayer and Bible study during these difficult times. But, some of us don't expect the Holy Spirit to do anything for us. When we do have answers to our prayers or get a revelation from the Word, thrill and amazement carry us for a while. Then the crisis is over, and we coast along until we are desperate again. Does this sound familiar? It is for most Christians. We don't know anything about the Holy Spirit as comforter. I want to share a personal experience of the comfort of the Holy Spirit.

Our son was born prematurely, so his first few months were difficult. Although he grew in strength and began to walk and talk within the normal timeframe, I was still fearful about his health. When he was two, we went to a family reunion about three hundred miles from home. The climate there was hot and very humid, unlike the climate we were used to. He began to develop a cough and an irregular breathing pattern. It grew worse, so by the second evening, we decided to start the trip back home. We traveled at night because it would be cooler. We had driven for about two hundred miles when we had to stop at an emergency clinic for help. The doctor there gave him a shot and told us to drive home as quickly as possible. He was getting worse by the hour. His breathing was labored, and he cried continually. When we arrived at our home town, his doctor met us at the hospital and began treatment. The x-ray showed his lungs were under such stress they were shaped like small light bulbs. For the next few days, he stayed under an oxygen tent and only came out for a diaper change or feeding. He would crawl back under the tent if we took him out for anything else. I was exhausted by the end of the second day, so my husband told me to go home, shower and sleep awhile. I did as he said. Later, as I laid on the bed praying, I asked God why he had given me a child if he was only going to take him away. He answered, "He isn't going to die!" I had never heard the Spirit speak to me like that before. Instantly, the pressure and worry were gone! My son would live.

You see, even though I had been saved at the age of fourteen, I did not know Jesus would comfort me personally by the Holy Spirit. This experience made me more aware of His presence. A few years later we attended a Bible study down the street from our house. I wanted to have a deeper relationship with Jesus, and it was at this Bible study that I asked Him to baptize me in the Holy Spirit. Immediately, I spoke with other tongues in my new prayer language. As I studied the Word after that, revelation of Jesus began to explode within me! The Holy Spirit was broadening my understanding of who Jesus was. This baptism gave me the power to live the Christian life as Jesus intended.

Luke 11:13 NKJV:

"If you then, being evil, know how to give good gifts to your children, how much more will your heavenly Father give the Holy Spirit to those who ask Him!"

Jesus sent the Holy Spirit to strengthen us and help us stop our roller coaster style of living. The Holy Spirit gives us power to break free and stop these emotional swings in our walk. With this baptism, the Spirit creates in us a balanced and godly lifestyle. He gives us the power to walk the Spirit-led life. Since Jesus the Baptizer is the one who baptizes us in the Holy Spirit, we have nothing to fear. We ask Jesus for this gift, and when we receive it, the first evidence we have is usually our new prayer language, tongues.

There are those who think tongues is of the devil, but this is not true. The devil cannot understand tongues, therefore he fights it with lies. Our new prayer language leaves him at a great disadvantage. The Spirit Himself is praying through us in the language of men and of angels. Then, as we study, our revelation knowledge of the Word expands dramatically, and therefore, the power to live the Spirit-filled life is released in us. Our influence expands as we walk with the Holy Spirit, being led step by step.

With the Holy Spirit operating in us, we can begin to know Jesus on a more intimate level. The Holy Spirit always glorifies Jesus. He makes us aware of our Deliverer, Counselor, Provider and Friend. As we come into a greater understanding of Jesus' many attributes, we come to know His relationship to mankind. His love is revealed to us at its height, depth, width and length. This is where the gift of influence comes into play. Through our knowledge of this great love, we become His hands, His feet and His voice within our spheres here on earth. Through the Holy Spirit, our confidence to operate in the fullness of our influence grows. If we don't understand our relationship to Jesus, or the many facets of His names, we will not understand our relationship to people. **Our expectation for successful influence with people is in direct proportion to our intimate relationship with Jesus through the Holy Spirit.**

We must develop confidence in our roles and stop holding back. To do this, we have to realize we are loved and accepted. Jesus isn't waiting for us to perform well or make our mark on the world in order to qualify. It's by His grace and mercy we qualify, not of our own works. He gives us His righteousness. We don't earn it. This scripture gives us a view from His perspective.

In Jeremiah 1:5, we see He knows us before we are ever in the womb, before we are born. He knew all along we would be women. We are who He expected us to be. Jesus wants to use us. We can sit back and watch others go forward, influencing things around them for good. Or we can take a deep breath and move forward by faith, knowing He's right there to guide, strengthen, encourage and bless us through the Holy Spirit.

Women have special abilities. With the Holy Spirit's help, a woman can move into areas few men ever see. We are invited to share a neighbor's heartache, a child's tears or a teenager's broken heart. The Lord can use our spiritual side to "hear" another's heart or to "see" another's wounds. The nurturing aspect of our spiritual makeup will open doors everywhere. He will operate through us to heal others as we rely on the Holy Spirit. As we grow in our understanding, we become more like Him in our thinking and behavior.

Philippians 2:13 NKJV:

"For it is God who works in you both to will and to do for His good pleasure."

Bit by bit, our minds are renewed by His Word. Under the surface, in our subconscious, He is working. The Spirit is busy changing us from within! The part of this scripture that stands out to me is the phrase "for His good pleasure." He knows exactly where we need to adjust in order to come into alignment with His purpose for our lives. He is actually working on us to please Himself! Who could ask for a better deal than that? The creator Himself is repairing us!

We will be amazed at what He will do for us and through us. Because His grace is sufficient, we can humbly move forward to do everything He leads us to do by the Spirit. It's His work, by His power, in His timing. We don't have to worry about being off the path as long as we seek Him. He will guide us through the mazes of life and put us at the exact place Jesus desires us to be.

The greatness of Jesus' work is shown to us in His many names. They paint a picture of the Father's heart concerning us. He had a plan from the beginning for redemption; it will take a lifetime to understand the complete work He did for us. The facets of Jesus' names reveal the areas where we needed redemption. Jesus is Redeemer, Lord, Savior, Healer, Counselor, Warrior, Baptizer, Friend, Provider, Conquering King, Alpha and Omega. This is who Jesus is to us as revealed by the Holy Spirit.

Chapter 4

What Changed for Us at the Cross?

Now that we've seen who Jesus is to us, we can better see what changed for us as women at the cross. In this chapter, we will explore the changes that have occurred and the impact these changes have made on our ability to influence the world around us. Can we identify these changes? It's very important that we do.

2 Corinthians 5:17 NKJV:

"Therefore, if anyone is in Christ, he is a new creation; old things have passed away; behold, all things have become new."

Since all things have become new, how do we see ourselves? Are we still following the list of rules we had, or are we performing the old duties we have always done? Let's see how this scripture applies to these. We are no longer under the restrictions placed on us by religious law. We are now under the law of love or grace brought to us at the cross by Jesus. There is a great difference in the two. The old covenant represented the law, while the new covenant represents grace and the relationship with Jesus and the Father. Law versus grace. Let's see what the difference means for us.

From our position in grace, many things are available to us that were not available under the law. This gives us a great advantage when we try to influence things around us. With the law in place, we could not speak in church, do any work on the Sabbath day, teach men, or even be out in public during our monthly cycle. All this was done away with at the cross. Now we are free to speak, work, teach and be out in public regardless of the time of the month.

It's much like comparing daylight to darkness. It's so important we understand the price Jesus paid to gain our freedom from the law. Every aspect of His death bought freedom for us. The thorns on His head bought our peace of mind. The stripes on His body bought our healing. Each drop of blood He shed bought our freedom from the power of sin. Now we are free to stand in our position of righteousness knowing we don't have to make sacrifices to be in right standing with God. We stand in the righteousness of God by faith in Jesus Christ's complete work on the cross. It takes a while before we can comprehend this. When He said on the cross, "It is finished," He was saying everything that the law required of us was taken care of by Him.

2 Corinthians 5:21 NKJV:

"For He made Him who knew no sin to be sin for us, that we might become the righteousness of God in Him."

Under the law, we were continually conscious of sin, always being reminded that we must make sacrifices for our failures. To break one law meant we had broken them all. It was an impossible thing to be righteous. Now we do not have to atone for our sin, because Jesus was the sacrifice for all sin for all time. His love has been shed abroad in our hearts by the Spirit. Now we operate in the law of love from the heart instead of the law of requirements of the flesh.

Throughout history, women have been restricted in their activities and opportunities by both civil and religious laws. There are still some countries and religions allowing these restrictions to remain intact today. For instance, in nations practicing different sects of Islam, these restrictions exist. In some, women are required to wear clothing that covers their entire body, including their faces. The facial covering has only a small opening, which allows them to see out. It restricts their sight so much it causes damage to their eyes. Many women have permanent damage, even blindness, from this. We ask ourselves, "How can this be? Why doesn't someone do something to change this?" We can do something—bring in the gospel of Jesus. He brings life and freedom to all those who believe on Him. The Word says:

Romans 1:16 NKJV:

"For I am not ashamed of the gospel of Christ, for it is the power of God to salvation for everyone who believes, for the Jew first and also for the Greek."

2 Corinthians 3:6 NKJV:

"Who also made us sufficient as ministers of the new covenant, not of the letter but of the Spirit; for the letter kills, but the Spirit gives life."

Religion is always at odds with grace. We might think we are free here in America from such things, but we have religious restrictions too. Some are taught

What Changed for Us at the Cross?

to wear clothing to the ankles, hair to the waist, or no makeup. These requirements all have to do with the flesh, not the heart. Law only deals with the flesh of man, while grace deals with the spirit of man, which is the heart. When Jesus taught, He never mentioned clothing, hair, or makeup in regard to a restriction. He was interested in the heart of the person.

There are many other restrictions impairing our spiritual freedom. Can we identify them? Are we free to see what we need to see, or are we allowing restrictions to blind us to the opportunities we have to get involved? Let's take a look at some of these.

We might have the idea we might miss what God is saying to us or we might make someone angry if we voiced our opinion about a matter. Do we have "religious" clothing over our hearts that is impairing our spiritual vision? I think many of us do. How we were raised and the type of religious training we've had can be affecting us. We have allowed these to speak loudly to us when making decisions. Even public opinion rings in our heads when we're asked to do something out of the ordinary. Sound familiar? Well, the devil is good at his job. These familiar voices and reminders come to us from the enemy when the Holy Spirit is tugging at our hearts to influence a situation.

Jesus was continually going against the traditions of men and public opinion. At the cross, His sacrifice ensured that the church would have the opportunity to walk in complete freedom from these. We are free to make decisions from the heart now. It's up to us to fulfill the purposes and plans He has for us. Let freedom reign! We are free from the dos and don'ts of tradition. Now we can BE! To BE means to rest in what He did for us at the cross. From His perspective, He sees that we ARE complete, fruitful, powerful, capable and anointed. Each thought going through our minds should line up with His perspective of us. We can do this, ladies!

Hebrews 4:16 NKJV:

"Let us therefore come boldly to the throne of grace, that we may obtain mercy and find grace to help in time of need."

Jesus gave us access to the Holy of Holies. We must take full advantage of this access. What a great opportunity we have! We can move into the things God has for us as we accept our place, free ourselves and respond to the Spirit by entering into His rest. In our newfound freedom, we must remember more is required of us. We must show by the character

What Changed for Us at the Cross?

of honor, dignity and service what this grace has brought to our lives. It must be demonstrated in our families first. Our husbands and children should be the first partakers of it. Then we can let it spread to our workplaces and communities. Grace is a gift, and it must be shared with others. After all, it is the good news of the gospel.

With the coming of Jesus, women were brought into the light the same as men. Jesus instructed the women along with the men and gave them opportunities to serve Him. The Scriptures show Him using women to spread the gospel of His kingdom. One great example of this is the woman at the well. She was one of His first evangelists! Many times women are seen in the Scriptures anointing Him, serving Him and hosting His meetings. Grace and truth came to us through Jesus. By His grace to us, we can move into areas we normally don't venture into. Restrictions were not placed on us by Him but through ourselves or others. In order for us to influence everything around us for good, we must break free from these restrictions.

In conclusion of our look at the cross, we can see ourselves and our purposes differently. There is no more sacrifice for sin, because Jesus was the final and complete sacrifice. He was the Lamb of God, and His blood was sufficient to abolish the penalty of sin for all time. The law was done away with, so sin no longer is being imputed. We have a new covenant with God. The requirements of the old have been fulfilled. Jesus fulfilled every one of them. The division between man and God has been removed in Jesus' death. We have access to Him and can boldly go before His throne with our petitions. We are priests and kings unto our God now!

Chapter 5

What Is Total Reconciliation?

When I hear the word "reconciliation," I think of reconciling accounting books or my checkbook. Both have to be reconciled or balanced to keep us out of the red. This is what God Himself did for us. We were fallen and without hope of redemption. We had no hope of ever bringing the "books" into balance on our own. There was nothing we could do to reconcile them. He made a way for us where there was none.

What does reconciliation look like? Have we accepted its reality? First, let's define it. According to W.E. Vines' *An Expository Dictionary of New Testament Words*, it means the following: to change, exchange; hence, of persons, to change from enmity to friendship, to reconcile. With regard to the relationship between God and man, the use of this and connected words shows that primarily reconciliation is what God accomplishes, exercising His grace towards sinful man on the ground of the death of Christ in propitiatory sacrifice under the judgment due to sin, such as 2 Corinthians 5:21, where both the verb and the noun are used. By reason of this, men, in their sinful condition and alienation from God, are invited to be reconciled to Him; that is to say, to change their attitude and accept the provision God has made, whereby their sins can be remitted and they themselves can be justified in His sight in Christ.

Of course, a definition is only that unless we "knowingly" experience it. It's important to fully understand the provision made for us so we can benefit from it. Revelation knowledge of our full salvation by the Holy Spirit will bring us to the understanding of total reconciliation. God accomplished it through the sacrifice of Jesus. Knowing what it means versus being what it says is the problem we have. We know in part what Jesus did on the cross for us physically, but we don't fully understand what it meant for us both physically and spiritually. In order for us to appreciate what He did, the gray areas in our understanding have to be enlightened by the Word of God through the Holy Spirit. **He has brought us back to the state of being man had before the Fall.** Now our fellowship with Him can be experienced to the fullest. We are no longer alienated from Him except in our own minds.

What Is Total Reconciliation?

For years we have been limited in our effective influence through misunderstanding what was done for us at the cross. We have let old ways of thinking and bad doctrine keep us out of touch with the benefits of the cross. The darkness we have walked in all our lives seems to cling to us for a long time as we start the renewal process. We are unfamiliar with His total acceptance, total love and total faithfulness. God's goodness seems foreign to us at first. It seems too good to be true! It is true, however. He sees us as members of His immediate family, joint heirs with Christ.

It takes us a while before we can embrace all this good news. But, now we are on our way. Our attitudes are being washed by the Word of God. We see them in holy light now, and we want them changed. Layer upon layer of old ways begin to melt away. The process of healing our thought life has begun. Imagine for a few minutes you are in the state of complete restoration with no sin and no remembrance of it. It's breathtaking! Total freedom from past experiences and failures. This is what reconciliation with God looks like. No shadows or fears anywhere! It might take us time to come to this thinking, but it's there waiting for us all the same. Our influence on those around us can be full and complete.

Application of the truth of reconciliation to our daily life starts at home. We can take steps one at a time to infiltrate our homes with this truth. Our influence here is very important. As we adapt, the effect will be wonderful in our families. As parents and relatives, it is important to teach the children how to come to proper conclusions in their thinking. We can speak with confidence by the power of the Holy Spirit into their lives. In the past, our confidence was seriously undermined by our ignorance of full salvation. Now that is taken care of.

We understand the revelation of our influence. We know who we are as women. We know who Jesus Christ is to us. We know what changed for us at the cross. And we know what being fully reconciled means. Now how do we put it all into action?

Chapter 6

How Do We Get Started?

All of us have had someone in our lives who was influential. Usually we think of them with high regard. Our memories of certain events will bring up thoughts of teachers, friends, or relatives who impacted our lives positively or negatively. We want to influence others and create positive memories in their lives. Let's see how we can do this.

Here are some of my childhood experiences with people of influence. Notice how the adults were involved with us, and see if you can apply any of these stories to your own life.

There were many lively children on Hughes Street. We would start playing early in the morning and come in the house only to eat or have a bathroom break. Most of the mothers on our street were "stay at home" moms. We would play for a while at one home then take off down the block to someone else's. If we became a nuisance there, we would be asked to go play somewhere else.

Play was an important part of my development. Since I was the youngest in my family and the only girl, I was spoiled. My brothers were much older than I, so the neighborhood children helped me learn how to interact with others my age. It didn't take too many times of being sent home before I learned to share or that pushing others was not acceptable. The mothers on our street seemed to have a similar understanding of what was proper behavior and what was not. For the most part, these mothers were morally sound with character and values. Mothers and playtime seemed to go together like peanut butter and jelly. As we were guided in our play, the issues we had with each other were talked about and resolved properly most of the time.

From the age of four to adolescence, I was very impressed with the inner workings of the families on my street. I observed how one family would pray together. Another one would play board games together. There was one large family who always went to church together. They also had chickens and a milk cow in a pen at the edge of the canyon at the end of our street. This family would occasionally take me to Sunday school with them. My parents were believers too, but they didn't attend church at that time. God always had people, especially women, who guided me toward Him. Hughes Street was a place of adult/child interaction. It was a wonderful place to grow up!

In the summer, our evenings were spent outside playing until bedtime. Our parents would sit on the porch in lawn chairs sometimes to watch. We would gather to play "gray wolf," which is hide-n-seek after dark! We would decide whose front porch would be home base then turn on the porch light there. The person who was "it" would count to twenty-five while the rest of us scattered like roaches and hid under bushes and behind cars. Then "It" would start looking for us. I remember laying on my stomach under a hedge with my heart beating so hard I could hear it. I would ask myself, "Should I make a run for home base or not?" Then I would take off running for that lighted porch with all my might! Sometimes I would make it home free, but other times my legs wouldn't move fast enough, and I would be caught before reaching safety.

What a thrill it was! I learned how I should respond both when I was caught and if I made it to safety. Being a part of the "herd" of Hughes Street taught me many things. I learned quickly not to cry when I didn't get my way. I learned to say thank you, please and excuse me. I learned to help other children who might not run as quickly as I. I learned all this through interaction with my peers and the adults who were involved during playtime.

I realize these stories are simple, but they do show how easy it is to become the influence in a child's life. The main thing I realize now when I think of these childhood stories is the amount of adult influence we had in our lives. We knew their names, and they knew ours. They would help us if we fell or hurt ourselves. They were there! They were involved and interested in us. We could count on them. They made themselves available to talk, to laugh and to enjoy daily events on our street. My life was shaped by their influence. Today it's hard to find an adult outside where the children are playing. I am truly thankful to God they were in my life.

We can still influence the children in our neighborhoods today. It just takes a little preparation and effort on our part. Meeting with the neighbors and discussing the possibilities is one way to get started. From there we can begin to branch out into the community. Many employers have an interest in sponsoring sports groups for children. This might be a place for our involvement. Remember, it's for the purpose of influence we are doing this. There are many who will not understand, but we don't let that impact our influence. We are on a mission from God. Our influence in these groups can make the difference in the lives of both children and adults. With our knowledge of God's love for us and all humanity, we can move into any group and influence it for good. We are His ambassadors. God has given us the Great Commission.

Matthew 28:18–20 NKJV:

And Jesus came and spoke to them, saying, "All authority has been given to Me in heaven and on earth. Go therefore and make disciples of all the nations, baptizing them in the name of the Father and the Son and of the Holy Spirit, teaching them to observe all things that I have commanded you even to the end of the age."

We can see clearly here that we are to be VERY involved with people. It's who we are in this world as believers that will change things around us. Our influence is guaranteed by the Lord. With the guidance of the Holy Spirit and our willing hearts, much can be accomplished. Our commitment to making changes is what it takes; first changing ourselves then changing the atmosphere of the world around us.

I remember one summer when the Baptist church in town had a Summer Recreation Week. I enrolled. A nice lady from the community held craft sessions during that week, and I learned many things from her. You see, I was being drawn to Jesus by the Holy Spirit at that time in my life. She was used by God as an influence because she was a Christian. Her sweet and kind attitude with us was wonderful. She encouraged us as we painted and made attempts to create something worth taking home to our mothers. She would start each afternoon session with a verse from the Bible, and we didn't mind a bit.

Summer was usually one hot day after another with few distractions from our ordinary lives. But, this summer was different. We had someone blessing us and teaching us about Jesus. I finished my project, and it turned out beautifully! I was so pleased to give it to my mother. It was two painted toy violins wired to a framed piece of velvet. Of course, it was just some paint, cloth, two toy violins, a wooden frame and wire, but to me, it was more. It was a doorway

How Do We Get Started?

Jesus used to enter into my heart. Later on, in the fall, the same church had a youth revival with a guest evangelist. I attended one session and received Jesus as my Lord and Savior. One young woman's influence in combination with the Word of God and the Holy Spirit had made this possible. All it took was her availability. The rest was simple. **God uses our availability to promote the Gospel of Jesus Christ.**

Let's get started now. We have wasted too many years in our doubts and fears. We have a garden to plant in the hearts of children and others. Ladies, let's start wherever we find ourselves today because it begins with us. Our first goal is to change how we view ourselves as women. If we don't see us, how can we see them? **People need to know there is a place in our hearts for them, a place no one else can fill. They need to know we need them.**

There are young women and men who need our loving touch, kind words, or simple friendship. We can impact their lives. We can help change their futures. The gift of influence is powerful, and with God's help, we can make it work in this day and age. I realize this must sound like a lot of work to some of you, but it actually isn't. The patience and wisdom to start influencing things with our families and friends comes from God Himself. His grace is sufficient.

Our main focus must be our relationship with Him. He is the source of the power and the ability to get it done. He will set the pace and the timing. As we relate to Him and give Him this place in us, we will see things begin to change. Our ability to "see" will be increased by the Holy Spirit so we can make precision strikes at problem areas! We will go directly to the spot that needs our attention without wasting time and energy. God is in this with us, and He wants it to work more than we do!

Prayer is a big part of the preparation for success. A routine time set aside for prayer and Bible study is so important. If we are not diligent to set time aside, the enemy will steal it from us. My time is early Saturday mornings while the house is quiet and no one has stirred. This time has proven to be the most beneficial for me. Some of my friends set aside the time when they are getting ready for work. Regardless of when you choose to have a quiet time with the Lord, it will benefit you and those you are purposing to influence.

For most of us, confidence is a problem. We don't see ourselves as worthy enough, bright enough, or qualified enough to impact others' lives. This is where we must identify with Christ. It isn't about our qualifications. It's about His. He has chosen us.

It doesn't matter how educated or how prosperous we are. It does matter, however, how submitted we are to Him. Some of the most influential people in my life weren't pretty, schooled, or wealthy. They simply loved.

The most beautiful women I have ever seen display kindness, gentleness, patience and joy. Their beauty comes from within. Their character has been reshaped by relating to Jesus. These attributes are called fruit of the Spirit in Galatians 5:22. Our beauty in the Spirit and influence can beneficially affect those around us. This kind of beauty is attractive. Jesus' beauty came from His relationship with the Father, much like ours does. We can attract people in the same way He did. Love, joy, peace, patience, kindness, goodness, and self-control in us will work for the kingdom's sake too. We shine in this dark world!

Isaiah 60:1–3 NKJV:

"Arise, shine; for your light has come! And the glory of the Lord is risen upon you. For behold, the darkness shall cover the earth, and deep darkness the people: But the Lord will arise over you, and His glory will be seen upon you. The Gentiles shall come to your light, and kings to the brightness of your rising."

Yes, your light shines in the eyes of all who see you. We are the light of the world. It's hard to imagine the creator of the universe using us to bring the light of the gospel to others, but He is. It was His plan all along. So let's get to it!

Influence, influence, influence! Every cashier, every sales person, every boss, every child and every other person you meet should realize you are different. They should remember having met you. The display of the attributes of God in your life can change the atmosphere in any office or business. Get ready for God's favor with man, just like Jesus had. The brightness of your rising will attract them like flies to pie! Before you know it, they will ask questions about the reason for your joy, peace and kindness. The opportunities to witness will be limitless.

The hardest place you'll ever find to witness will be in your own family. They have watched you go through changes in the past and really want to "wait and see" before asking any questions. But, that doesn't matter. Eventually, the overwhelming evidence will get through to them. You have become a woman of influence with all the grace and dignity of Jesus Himself. Rest in being who you are. Don't worry about their opinion; it will change eventually.

If you have been the type who withdraws from relationships or from conflict of any type, becoming involved might take a little longer. But, don't give up. As you seek the Lord and rely on His grace, He will develop a love for people in you that will overcome your fears of relationship. He loves people, and so will you! City Council, PTA and Meals on Wheels are just a few places to get involved. There are many other places to venture into. It will be fun and adventurous for you. Only you and Jesus will know the extent of your fears. Let Him help to guide you through it. Remember, you are more than a conqueror through Christ who strengthens you.

The End

Thank you for spending this time with me. I know the Lord has great plans for your life.

Everyone you know will be blessed because of your influence through honor, dignity and service.

www.ingramcontent.com/pod-product-compliance
Lightning Source LLC
Chambersburg PA
CBHW061509040426
42450CB00008B/1541